SECURING BUSINESS DATA

ESTABLISHING A CORE VALUE FOR DATA SECURITY

NATHAN JAMES NEIL

Copyright © 2015

More resources and information available for free at:

NathanNeil.com

WHY I WROTE THIS BOOK

Over the last several years, as a technology consultant, I have observed many businesses fall victim to data breaches, malware, and viruses that cause damage to their business. Everyday, the media outlets discuss a new data breach and the millions of people who will be affected by it - but what we do not hear is a plan of action for how our businesses can secure their infrastructure and data. My objective for writing this book is to provide you with an understanding of how to make data security a core value.

Towards the end of 2014, I began sharing information and advice with listeners on a local talk radio station. From researching data breaches, both internal and external, I was able to compile a list of key components that businesses need to establish to secure their data.

Some breaches can be prevented with hardware like firewalls and spam filters, but from my observations, many companies affected had excellent technology infrastructure in place. Even if you have the best technology in place with the strongest antivirus and a well-maintained firewall, the human element of your business still remains the proverbial wildcard in regard to security. The key element to this book is giving you the steps that your business should take in order to protect data and establish an internal value for data security.

Data breaches occur on a continuous basis and, I believe, we take for granted the value of our information.

WHY YOU SHOULD READ THIS BOOK

This book is designed to help managers, technology coordinators, and human resources professionals to have all the procedures in place to protect their businesses from data breaches. The first chapters of this book look at the hardware and software side of protecting your business or organization. It's important to have a good foundation of security in terms of hardware appliances and security software.

Many security consultants focus on attacks that come from external forces. External attacks are a substantial threat; according to the Online Trust Alliance these attacks account for 40% of breaches with the loss of personal information. Many foreign governments target U.S. intellectual property and businesses. More recently, terrorist organizations have targeted defacing business web pages to distribute their propaganda.

While having established hardware and software elements is important, many businesses miss securing the human element of data security. You may have had your business secured from externally caused breaches, but another 29% are caused either accidentally or maliciously by employees or contractors. Most often, these internal breaches are caused by mistake, miseducation, or misdirection. This book covers those topics to help educate staff, put proper policies into place, and ensure that you are protected on the inside.

This book takes a multi-level approach to data security and can apply to multiple business departments.

Special Thanks and Dedication

I would like to thank a few people who have given me the inspiration, support, and mentorship over the last few years. There are so many I would like to mention, but there are a few I would remiss not to single out.

Special thanks to my wonderful wife, Cierra Neil, for supporting me in not only my career path, but also my pursuit to share my knowledge with others.

Thank you to my high school mentor, Mathern Mellott. I will never be able to thank you enough for believing in me, my research, and for always driving me to come up with new creative ideas.

During my college years, I found strong inspiration and leadership from Dr. Marsh, who was a mentor, friend, and among the first to introduce me to cyber security. Thank you for your support and continued friendship.

I also want to thank my boss and business partner, James Sulfare, Jr. You not only mentored me, but helped me grow into the business leader and technology consultant that I am today. Thank you for all of the knowledge and wisdom that you have shared.

I would also like to dedicate this book in memory of my dear friend Grant MacKenzie, who was taken away too soon. Not a day goes past that I do not think of you.

LEGAL DISCLAIMER

The content of this book expresses the views and opinions of the author in establishing a strong security policy for your businesses data. It does not necessarily reflect the views and opinions of the author's business entities, affiliates, or partners. It is designed to provide information and outline good practices for establishing a core value for data security.

The author is not a human resources specialist nor an attorney and is not a substitute for seeking the advice of your attorney or human resources partner. This book provides outlines of what the author believes to be best-practices advice for policies and procedures, but is not intended or should be taken as legal advice. This book and its author only intend on providing self-help information for your direction for employee policies, security policy, and other subjects that relate to data security.

Table of Contents

CHAPTER 1

THE WALL

In the 14th century, The Great Wall in China was revived in order to protect China from Mongolian tribes. This is ironic as now, in the 21st century, we must put up technological "walls" to protect our own electronic data from countries such as China, Russia and others. It is amazing to me that, even with the knowledge we have in regard to active external threats, we still let our guard down and fail to practice proactive measures to keep our data safe.

In August 2015, it was reported that China stole US corporate secrets, intellectual property, and military data in over 600 successful cyber-attacks. If that's the amount of breaches that were detected, just imagine how many were not. It's mind blowing. This chapter is dedicated to establishing some metaphorical "Great Walls" that businesses can put up to protect themselves from intruders.

OFFICE OF PERSONNEL MANAGEMENT BREACH

The US Government's Office of Personnel Management had personal data of close to 14 million people breached in an attack. According to news outlets, this attack was executed by the Chinese government. Several factors lead to this being a relatively easy target for the hackers. A lot of the measures that we are going to discuss throughout out this book were simply, and inexplicably, not in place.

One of the technology flaws was a very lenient security policy that did not have encryption measures in place. This would have added another layer of security or 'wall' for the attackers to get through before acquiring the personal data of millions.

Think of encryption like this. When you mail a postcard, anyone can see the information on it. When you mail a letter, the contents remain unseen until the recipient opens it. Encrypted data is like a letter in an envelope. Unencrypted data is much like the postcard or an open book.

There were also human resources and technology management measures that did not exist as well that would have added additional levels of security.

One major flaw was that the Office of Personnel Management (OPM) did not have any information security staff or contractors until 2013. This is a huge issue. If your company cannot afford a full-time staff member that specializes in information security, learn from this mistake and budget to have a contractor to come in to conduct quarterly security audits on your data practices. It is worth every dime.

OPM also did not have an inventory list of where their workstations and servers were located and what outside systems were connected. If you are a business owner and have technology assets, it is imperative to know where your systems are and who has access to them.

Further, workers that accessed the network remotely didn't need to use a second form of user authentication. Basically, if an attacker could get a list of user IDs and run an attack using commonly used passwords, they could essentially walk through the metaphorical front door, take what they want, and disappear.

It was also rumored that OPM did not have antivirus and antimalware protection on a few of their key systems, which would have been an additional obstacle for hackers to maneuver around.

The OPM breach is a huge failure in both technology policy, device management, and general security practices. The OPM breach provides a great transition into the rest of this chapter as we look at 'walls' - both hardware and software - that we can put up to prevent most breaches from outside intruders. It also provides us with great reference points as we begin to dive deep into security and explore crucial policies that managers, technology coordinators, and human resource professionals need to establish in order to address the human element that contributed to this breach.

THE FIREWALL APPLIANCE

It is my goal to keep this book fairly low tech, since many readers may be business managers, owners, or human resource staff that do not have specific knowledge in information technology. I am going to do my best in these next few categories to keep it easy to understand by providing resources to take to your technology providers to ensure that your business or organization meets the level of compliance that this book outlines to achieve.

Your first 'Great Wall' to block malicious intruders is not one of block and stone like the Great Wall of China that was used to prevent the Mongolian tribes from attacking, but rather a hardware and software appliance that provides the first layer of security. What I am referring to is your firewall.

What is a firewall? A firewall is typically a physical appliance at the front end of your network. This appliance has software that monitors incoming and outgoing traffic. It is basically the air traffic controller of what leaves and comes into your network. Every business and organization needs a firewall regardless of the level of security that their industry requires.

Without a firewall, there is no way to control what goes in or out. We call these inbound and outbound requests. Without a firewall, there is no protection from software or malware.

There are many capabilities that various firewall manufacturers provide and it is important to consult your technology staff or contractor to see what firewall best fits the size and needs of your organization. A few questions that are good to ask to your technology provider are in the check list in figure 1a.

A key firewall component that many technology professionals do not take into consideration is whether or not the product can handle the size of your business. As you add both staff and workstations, it is important to have your technology staff or consultant to work with the firewall manufacturer to ensure that it meets your organizations size requirements. Otherwise, it could hinder performance, slow network speeds, or become overwhelmed and ineffective.

Many organizations do not realize that the software on a firewall expires and requires a license. Updates are required. Most subscriptions for updates come in 1, 3, and 5 year packages. It is crucial to know when your update license expires and make sure to renew.

The checklist in figure 1a is an excellent resource for managers and directors to use to ask of the technology staff to ensure that there are no vulnerabilities on this front.

Figure 1a. Firewall Security Questionnaire

Firewall Security Questionnaire	YES	NO
Is the Firewall Firmware up to date?		
Are the software updates installed?		
Is there a list of ports that are open?		
Are unused ports blocked from requests?		
Is our update license current or expired?		
Will we need to renew our license soon?		
Does the firewall meet the current requirements for the size of our business?		
Do users use a VPN or Remote Access to access company resources?		
Are we using the latest in VPN security?		

Antivirus & Antimalware

If you work in technology, you often cannot go a business day without a user contracting a virus or malware on their computer. It happens more often than it should. There are procedures that we will examine in a later chapter to help alleviate the human element, but frequently there are issues on the technology side of things that prevent the business or organization from having a strong level of protection against it.

Amazingly, one thing we still see is that businesses do not have antivirus installed on the computer. Not having antivirus is just asking for trouble. Installing an antivirus is an easy way to help prevent a breach. We also see businesses using free residential antivirus for their business. If you are using AVG free home edition for your business, shop for a business level solution - now.

Many businesses look for free solutions to reduce their costs, but they must look at security a little differently. If you have a safe filled with millions of dollars, are you going to hire a guard with an unknown background or are you going to pay a proven guard that has experience in securing safes and insuring that they are not cracked?

A data breach can cost thousands to millions of dollars. Sixty percent of businesses that report breaches are out of business within six months.

A virus or malware program that sends data to an unknown party is an easy way to have a data breach. This is why researching and having a proven antivirus with antimalware capabilities is so important. Don't look at it as a cost, but more of an investment to protect your business.

So what steps should you take in ensuring that you have taken the proper measures to protect your workstations from a virus? Easy. Find a reputable antivirus provider. Look at the cost of their service last, and the reputation of their service first.

Once you have selected and installed an antivirus suite, regularly check to make sure that it is installing the latest definitions. Definitions are essentially a list of known virus and malware codes for which your antivirus looks. Good antivirus should check for updates daily.

Additionally, you should have a quarterly review of your antivirus to see both how many viruses made it into the network and also how long you have before you need to renew your antivirus. If you have several viruses that hit your workstations, talk with your antivirus provider and technology staff to see how the virus got in and, depending on the circumstance, evaluate the possibility of finding another antivirus provider. With good antivirus software installed, an employee policy breach is often the reason a virus is able to get through the door.

Good employee policy and education is vital on preventing viruses, malware, ransomware, and other forms of malicious software. We will explore this later.

Spam Filter

There is a strong need to have a spam filter for your email system. Spam filtering keeps out emails that contain malware, phishing requests, advertisement spam, and other garbage. The first reason is because of efficiency. As your staff struggles to delete all of the spam messages, how much time are they wasting? In addition, the likelihood of an employee accidentally opening an email with a virus or malware increases. Even with good policies in place, you cannot get frustrated with an employee that gets a virus through email because you failed to provide readily available tools that could have prevented it.

If you still host in-house, it is important to consider purchasing a spam-filter if you don't have one. Figure 1b is a checklist to follow in this evaluation.

Figure 1b. Anti-Spam Questionnaire

Anti-Spam Questionnaire	YES	NO
Do we have a spam filter?		
Are the latest software updates installed?		
Do we have an active license for our filter?		
Are staff reporting spam emails in their inbox?		
Will we need to renew our license soon?		
Does the spam filter meet the current requirements for the size of our business?		

If you do not host your own email systems, you do not need to worry about the above checklist because your service provider likely has one in place.

A lot of companies are migrating from having email systems on premise (in a company owned/managed datacenter) to the cloud. Companies that subscribe to Office 365 or Google Apps get spam filtering as part of the service agreement, which makes this aspect a lot more manageable for small companies. For those who still host your own email server or pay a smaller provider to host email, it is important to determine if you have a spam filter.

What we have seen from small hosting providers is that they do not have spam filtering services due to the cost. If you are in this category and host with a smaller low-cost alternative for hosted email, you should have a talk with your provider to see if you are getting anti-spam services. If they say they are, ask what service they are using. These are important questions and are vital to the security of your company. If the company is using nothing or an open source (free) solution, it may be time to have a management meeting to consider moving to a more secure provider. In addition you should ask them if they are using a secure socket layer (SSL).

SSL's are fairly affordable and necessary to encrypt traffic that goes over the web. If they do not have this and lack an anti-spam feature, I strongly would recommend you find a provider that does and migrate services.

During your quarterly security meetings, ask the following questions:

1. How many occurrences of spam in employees' inboxes have been reported?
2. Has this increased since the last review?
3. Are we satisfied with our level of spam protection or should we have a meeting with our service provider?

Keep in mind that it is next to impossible to eliminate all email spam, but having a very strong policy is essential.

CHAPTER 2

SECURE PASSWORDS

I often rant about the importance of secure passwords and good practices that go along with them. Passwords are a vital 'wall' between your data and it being in the wrong hands. The security practices outlined in this book provide multiple methods of barriers - both physical and virtual - that must be used to secure both our personal and business interests.

In 2013, it was estimated that 60% of all security breaches were due to the fact that organizations had weak passwords and weak password policies.

There are four key ways that hackers or others can get access to your credentials:

1. Guessing
2. Dictionary Attack/Brute Force
3. Stolen/Given in Trust

Do you use the name of your pet, spouse, or something else that is personal? A lot of people do. Very frequently, a lot of people also use very common passwords. It is important not to use personal details when setting your password. It is also important not to use commonly used passwords. These make it very easy for someone to gain access to your data and are almost like having no protection at all.

Chances are that you may be using one of these passwords:

1. 123456
2. Password
3. 12345
4. 12345678
5. Qwerty
6. 123456789
7. 1234
8. Baseball
9. Dragon
10. Football

This list was compiled by using the most commonly used passwords that were acquired from data breaches. These are also very likely passwords for people to guess and are also the first that are used in dictionary and brute force attacks.

Protect yourself by using passwords that are random letters, numbers, and special characters. My recommendation is that passwords be at least 8-12 characters long. A common method that outside intruders use to gain access is either a brute force or a dictionary attack.

A dictionary attack is an attack that uses the dictionary word list to generate possible passwords. This means that any word in the dictionary is very vulnerable to these attacks and why having a password of random letters, numbers, and special characters is so important.

Brute force attacks are very successful against short passwords. They continue to generate and try passwords with number and letter combinations to force the intruder's way into your system.

A password like abc123 can be broken in a matter of minutes because of the way brute force works. The best way to protect yourself from these attacks is to use long passwords with random letters, numbers, and special characters. This will provide a strong level of protection because a brute force attack would take a very long time before acquiring the correct password.

The more random and longer the better because it increases the number of possible combinations that it will have to run through which further increases the amount of time that this kind of attack would take to be successful.

While doing research for a morning radio segment, I set up a small website using WordPress. I created several login IDs using weak passwords. By using free tools that are widely available on the internet, I was able to acquire the passwords to all of the user accounts in under five minutes. This isn't intended to scare you, but rather make you understand how easy it is for a bad actor to gain access.

The third way - stolen or given in trust - is just as, if not more frequent of an occurrence than a hacker getting into your account. Many people that use strong passwords write them down and hide them under their keyboard or in their desk. Many of their coworkers are also aware of this. If a coworker wants to gain access to a target's email or acquire files under that persons account, the victim has left the keys in the safe.

In addition to a password being stolen in the workplace, some workers share their passwords with others. Whatever the reason, this is not a good practice because relationships, and people, can change.

EXAMPLE PASSWORD POLICY

As a guide for human resources and technology managers, I have put together a small how-to in establishing a company-wide password policy.

This policy in figure 2a is for a fictional company that I am going to refer to in this book. We will call this company ABC Consulting.

Figure 2a

ABC Consulting Password Policy

At ABC Consulting, we must have a strong commitment to security as part of our core values in securing our intellectual property and client data. To achieve this goal, we have outlined the password policy for the company. We will ensure that the policy is being followed through our quarterly security audit. Any staff member not following the policy may be disciplined in correspondence with our violation terms.

1. Passwords must be greater than 10 characters in length
2. Passwords may not be commonly used words from the dictionary or have personal meaning
3. Passwords must consist of random numbers, letters, and symbols
4. The use of both capital and lower case characters is required
5. Passwords must be memorized and cannot be written down or stored in a file and/or online software
6. Passwords must not be shared with other staff members
7. Passwords for all company resources must be changed every three months
8. The repeat use of a password previously used is not permitted

Thank you for following these guidelines and helping ensure our core value of data security.

This is a good addition to any employee handbook. It may be a good idea to have meetings to review and instill these policies to help educate staff.

You want to make sure that your team has the knowledge and tools to fulfill the policy and, if a violation occurs, you need to discuss the following questions with the management team.

1. Did the staff member in violation understand our password policy and were they provided the information they needed?
2. Was this violation willful in that the employee had the education, but still went against the core values for data security?

You may notice that, in the example policy above, ABC Consulting outlined the password policy as part of their company's core values. I encourage you to do the same. If more businesses added the core value of wanting strong security for their intellectual property and client data, I believe that the number of breaches we hear about each day would decrease. Right now, it seems too many have a 'it won't happen to us' approach when it comes to data security.

It is also important not to just throw the policy out there. The number one complaint you will get while implementing a password policy is that memorizing them is too hard. It is important to assure staff that, while you understand, it is vital to the health of your organization. You certainly do not want to punish staff for forgetting their password, but they need to understand that the policy is in place to protect them and the company.

It is hard to be firm with those who willfully fail to adhere to the policy that you put into place. Termination seems so strong of a punishment, but keep in mind that a rogue employee can cause irreparable damage. I encourage you to discuss measures for punishing violators with your human resources department and legal counsel. My personal thought is that one violation is too many, but a firm warning with additional education for the first violation, may be sufficient.

CHAPTER 3

UPDATE, UPDATE, UPDATE!

When I first started working as a technology consultant just out of college, my mentor, boss, and now business partner taught me the importance of keeping systems up to date. This philosophy applies to all of the technology that you use. You may have noticed in both figures 1a and 1b that the checklists mention updates. This is because of the vital importance in keeping your company with the latest known security patches that are available. ALL products you use should receive regular updates. If they do not, ask why. Technology is constantly changing, new vulnerabilities are found daily, and your business should have the tools in place to prevent being another statistic by maintaining updates.

OPERATING SYSTEM UPDATES

One main topic I want to hit on is the use of operating systems that are not currently supported by the manufacturer. A good example is businesses that still utilize Windows XP and Vista. Microsoft no longer supplies security updates for these operating systems. The need to move away from them is vital. I understand that people are resistant to change and many people feel comfortable with Windows XP in particular, but in doing so you are leaving yourselves wide open to a variety of attacks.

In a test I did, I was able to remotely take control of a machine I setup with Windows XP and place malicious code into its core, preventing it from booting. The information on how to do such a nefarious thing is widely available on the internet. Anybody can do this. Your main concern here is not necessarily some sophisticated hacker, but more likely what is called a "script kiddie". A script kiddie by definition is a person who uses information found on the internet to attack a system yet are not sophisticated enough to execute these attacks on their own.

Since technology is rapidly changing, I encourage you to go to your operating system's website and see what its life cycle is. This applies not only to Windows, but also to Mac and Linux systems. A lot of the sites in recent months that are being defaced by terrorist organizations are no longer receiving updates from the operating system's provider.

In figure 3a, you can see the current end support dates for the most popular operating systems.

Figure 3a. Operating System Lifecycle

Operating System	End of Mainstream Support	End of Extended Support
Windows XP Service Pack 3	4/14/2009	4/08/2014
Windows Vista Service Pack 2	4/10/2012	4/11/2017
Windows 7 Service Pack 1	1/13/2015	1/14/2020
Windows 8.1	1/09/2018	1/10/2023
Windows 10	10/13/2020	10/14/2025

There are many other operating systems that your business may use that is not on this chart. Figure 3a focuses on operating systems that are popular for workstations and have lifecycle information widely available. If you use another Windows or Linux product, search its version in Google with "lifecycle" in the search to see what your support is for the product.

If you use Mac, contact Apple and ask them as they do not have information on their lifecycles public and tend to end support based on their products rather than software.

If you are using a product that is not currently under support from the provider, it is my strong recommendation that you either update or find an alternative.

Knowing your support cycle on your operating system is only the first step. Regularly installing updates and making sure your systems have all of the updates installed that are available is the next step.

As an example, Windows sends software patches or updates down weekly (every Tuesday). It is important that your technology department has measures to ensure that these updates are installed. This is a weekly task that is vital to the security of your company. Many managed service providers have means to automate these checks and balances through software that they use. In some circumstances, it may be viable to make sure employees install updates as part of maintaining a company-issued machine as part of employee policy.

In addition to workstations being updated with the latest OS patches, your servers also must be updated with the latest patches. For Windows Server users, these patches are also sent down weekly. If your technology department is currently using Windows Server 2003, it is no longer receiving support and your organization should discuss updating to a newer release. While licensing is expensive, a data breach will make that amount look paltry.

ENSURING WORKSTATION SECURITY

While java is frequently a morning drink enjoyed by many members of management and staff, it is also a software package that requires frequent updates. There are often reports of vulnerabilities in Java, but since a lot of the software business use rely on its framework, we cannot avoid using it. What is important is that your technology team keeps current with when new Java versions are released, as frequent as they may be, and install the latest versions on your company workstations.

With Java your technology team should be able to follow these guidelines:

1. Is the latest version of Java installed?
2. Are all old versions of Java removed?
3. Do we have a method of becoming aware as soon as a new version is released?

By asking these three questions, your organization should be better protected from outside issues with Java.

A Zero Day Attack is an attack that uses a vulnerability unknown to the software vendor. By following the guidelines above, you can ensure a high-level of safety from known issues. As discussed in the first chapter, implementing good antivirus can help minimize the risk from Zero Day Attacks.

Adobe, like Java, also sends down frequent updates for their software products like Flash, Adobe Reader, and others. Your technology department should follow similar steps like the ones suggested for Java to ensure that you have the latest versions of these programs and that all updates for known issues are installed.

Several technology and business managers recently have learned a lesson about keeping Adobe up to date recently. As I started writing this chapter, a headline popped up on my news feed that one of the largest Flash exploits ever was affecting Yahoo users. What happened was that hackers purchased advertising space on Yahoo Finance, News, and Sports, and inside of their ad was malware that would automatically execute when the user loaded the page. From there, the malware would search for old versions of Flash and use them to either take the computer's files ransom or use the computer as a bot to send traffic across the internet.

This is concerning since most people I have polled consider Yahoo a safe and reputable site. We need to be very cautious and make sure that we take measures to protect ourselves because a potential data breach can originate from places you would least expect. Around 6.9 billion users visit Yahoo in a month and Yahoo is unsure how many people were affected. While Yahoo should be proactive in monitoring what advertisements they serve up to people, the affected users would not have ran into an issue if they followed the policy outline in this chapter and updated their software.

Drivers are software that allows your computer to talk to the hardware that is installed on the workstation. While these can play a role in security they also play a role in system functionality. Computer manufactures typically release quarterly updates, which should be installed to ensure the longevity of your investment in the workstation.

Computer manufacturers like Lenovo for example, have excellent utilities to ensure the installation of the latest system drivers. As part of your quarterly review, you should also verify that the technology department has done its role in ensuring that the latest drivers are in place.

Chapter 4

WordPress, Websites & Hosting

Yes, WordPress has its own chapter here and it is strategically placed. We just learned about the importance of strong passwords and updates. Approximately 23% of websites in the world are using WordPress and, of that, 73% are vulnerable.

With any website, you should make sure that you keep the software that runs it updated and follow the guidelines regarding secure passwords.

Before I start talking about its vulnerabilities, I want to mention a few things. WordPress is a powerful content management tool that is very customizable with a variety of third party tools, which makes it great for deploying excellent websites for businesses and organizations. Most of the sites that I manage either personally or through our company utilize WordPress and see a great benefit from its ease of use, ability to be managed, and customization features. Well-maintained sites that use WordPress and follow the principles and policies outlined in this book will be able to see great benefit. It is when businesses fail to ensure good password policies, regular update plans and internal security that problems occur.

All too frequently, software gets the blame for problems when actually, the issue is internal. There are circumstances where software doesn't meet the internal requirements of a team but that's different. In the case of WordPress, it is often user action or lack of user action that causes issues to arise.

Before we start going through various policies that you should implement if your business uses a WordPress site, let's assume first that you are in the market for a website. There are nearly 300,000 companies that brand themselves specifically as website developers and even more businesses and contractors that also offer some sort of website development service.

The majority of these developers either utilize WordPress or a similar content management system (CMS). In some cases, creating a custom website is the best route. From my experience, most small, mid-size, and even enterprise level companies utilize WordPress because of its many features and levels of customization.

Below, figure 4a offers some good interview questions that you can use when interviewing prospective developers to determine if their security policy is in line with your core value for business data security. This is something often missed in the bidding and hiring process of developers.

Figure 4a. Web Developer Interview Questions
What content management system do you recommend?
Do you provide hosting or do we host the site?
What is your security policy and service level agreement? Are the systems being maintained with modern security and frequent updates?
Can we make content changes to our website?
After development, do you keep a login to our site and, if so, what is your company's security policy regarding logins and employee access?

Before I go in-depth in analyzing these questions, it is important to note that if you have an existing website and an existing provider, you should ask them similar questions. Often it is seen that data breaches of companies that have a good core value of security are breached through third party vendors. See figure 4b for follow-up questions to ask existing website providers.

Figure 4b. Existing Web Developer Questions
What content management system are we using and is it the most recent version?
Is hosting provided by your company or another vendor?
If you are hosting, what is your security policy and do we have a service level agreement? Are the systems being maintained with modern security and frequent updates?
Who has access to make content changes to our website?
What is your password and security policy regarding your access to our website?

As you can see, there are many similarities in the questions, but they are vital to establishing strong data security.

NEWEST SOFTWARE RELEASE

The first question on a content management system lets you know what software suite you are using and of what critical updates you need to be aware. If it is WordPress, you can easily check the current version of your site and match it with the latest release on the WordPress download page.

https://wordpress.org/download/

If you want to verify your existing website developers' answer, you can quickly find the version they imparted by going to http://mysite.com/readme.html and replacing mysite.com with your domain name. If you cannot access the page for your version, it could mean one of three things.

1. Your developer is very secure and removed the page to prevent possible hackers from seeing system versions.
2. Your developer removed the readme.html file, but does not maintain updates.
3. You are not really using WordPress.

Typically, it's going to be answer 1 or 2. In the case of answer 2, they may have had strong security intentions, but you may not have a service agreement that covers updates.

If the developer uses Joomla, Drupal or another CMS, you can go online to check and verify versions to ensure that what you are using or purchasing is starting with the most recent release.

In the case that the web developer creates a custom solution or has their own in house management system, there are several more questions to consider.

Do they regularly audit the security of their product? Large CMS solutions like WordPress and others receive frequent audits and updates to patch security holes. You want to make sure that if you are going to use their system that they will maintain it, ensure compliancy, and make sure that it fits with the most modern security standards.

Also, does the developer provide a way for you or your staff to update the content? This is important for several reasons. If you have a promotion you want to run or an important news release that you want to push out, you do not want your business waiting on them to find time to publish the information. In addition, what happens if the web developer goes out of business? If they maintain the updates, you more or less need to start over. There is also a cost element to custom-developed solutions, but for this book, we will only consider security the main factor of your decision.

WHO HOSTS THE SITE

The second question in figures 4a and 4b relates to who hosts the website. This is important. If you do not have the staff or the resources to maintain updates on the web server itself, you may want the developer to host your site. If the developer is hosting the site, you have a series of additional questions to ask. See figure 4c for hosting provider questions.

Figure 4c. Outside Hosting Questions
What is your company's policy for web server updates and at what frequency are they installed?
Does our company have a private server you are hosting or is it hosted with a group of other sites?
Does your company host through another provider? If so, what is their security policy regarding our data?
Do you take regular backups of our data?

There are, of course, many more questions to ask, but those outlined in figure 4c is a great core from which to work. The first question in regard to policy for server updates is important. The reason you should consider them as a host is because your staff and resources may not have time to maintain the level of security you are targeting. With that as a factor, you want to make real sure that they are preforming the updates to secure your data and also how frequently they install them. The answers will vary, but it should be fairly frequent. If they stumble answering this question or have to ask a supervisor, that, for me, would be a large, red flag. Their whole organization should absolutely be familiar with their security and update policy.

A good answer from them would be the following:

Given the nature of threats towards websites being defaced or infected with malware, we have a strong update policy and implement updates as we are aware of their release and stability.

Some developers may say they install them as frequently as they are released and that is ok, but I have always been cautious in installing server updates immediately as sometimes they can cause unforeseen issues.

It is not a bad practice to wait a reasonable amount of time to see if any issues with the update process are reported. What you may want to do is have someone who understands technology well at your organization call and ask them what versions they are running on their servers and if they are using older versions, ask why. This is important as some websites may not like the newer versions of software. If you need to pay to have some revamps done to your site to reach the new requirements, you will want to do that. What we see frequently is web developers who are afraid to go back and request payment for updating certain aspects of the site to maintain updates. No matter what you may need to do, making sure that they align with your data security core value is vital.

The next question you need to ask regarding web hosting is if the web developer hosts your site on its own private server - often referred to as Virtual Private Server (VPS) - or do they host all of their sites on a single server.

Shared hosting environments are dangerous. Many hosts use shared hosting environments to streamline management and keep internal costs down. The issue is that if one site that hosts has a security flaw, the other sites can often be easily compromised. There are practices that hosts can do to reduce this risk, but nothing is 100% secure in an environment with other sites.

XYZ Web Solutions Study

In my time as a technology consultant, we encountered several cases of web developers who hosted their sites on a single server. Let me give you an example of a real-world case. To protect the good reputation of those involved, we'll call this company XYZ Web Solutions.

XYZ Web Solutions used a shared hosting platform on a Windows Server. One of their clients had a special contact form that allowed the submission of files from a third party plugin. The plugin uploaded the files to the sites server to link in with the email that would be sent to the client. Through this plugin, a variety of hackers were able to upload malicious scripts. At first, it only affected one site, which directed traffic to several sites for the hackers to gain advertising revenues.

This was the beginning. After a period of time, another hacker uploaded malicious code that sniffed out the site's configuration files, giving them access to the database. From that point, the hackers were able to see and modify the configuration tables of about 25 other websites. After that exploit took place, another hacker group - through the doors the previous ones left open - was able to use the domains (www.example.com) of the hosted sites to send out spam email. All of this took place within days and quickly spread like an epidemic. Once XYZ Web Solutions noticed that their customers were being blacklisted and legitimate emails were no longer being received by the clients, we were hired to go in and perform a security audit, which uncovered the issues above.

Another point worth mentioning was, when we were called into review the status of the server, a hacker group that spreads radical Islam propaganda used the back doors to deface all of the websites to spread their propaganda. Many people would not realize how fast word of a vulnerable server spreads. By the time external signs of the hack were becoming visible, saving the server and correcting all of the back doors that were created was no longer a solution. We call this a complete compromise.

This left XYZ Web Solutions with two options – either move the sites to a new shared server or spend a lot of time and financial resources to move the sites to their own private servers.

My friend, mentor, and boss, James Sulfare, Jr. spent a lot of time analyzing the breach and putting together several policies to prevent future breaches for this web host. Many web development companies would have chosen the quick solution to launch a new shared server and migrate the data - which without policies in place and proactive measures - would result in further breaches. XYZ Web Solutions decided to make the commitment to establish a core value of data security, enact the policies that were recommended, and make the costly commitment to ensure that this did not happen again.

I am very proud of XYZ Web Solutions' decision. They had both internal and external factors that played into the breach. Some internal factors were not having strong password policies in place for their clients and not monitoring the software that their clients were uploading without their knowledge. Externally, they also had a key person at their company leave for another opportunity. Upon this person's departure, it was learned that he did not leave proper documentation on the configuration and security of the system.

XYZ Web Solutions had the best intentions. The sad reality was that the managed services provider employed quick fixes to address the immediate problems, but never addressed the source of the issue.

XYZ Web Solutions sincerely cared for their customers and were willing to do everything to ensure that the security issues would not occur again.

Every business has issues from time to time. I admire those that are transparent, honest, and admit they have a problem and work to address it. There are few that do this.

XYZ Web Solutions made the decision to migrate their clients to individual virtual private servers and had each site scanned and cleaned of vulnerabilities. With the number of sites XYZ Web Solutions hosted, this was a very time intensive process and costly for XYZ Web Solutions.

For XYZ Web Solutions, their customers were their number one priority. After some time, their customers were removed from blacklists and security to their data and sites was restored.

This case teaches many lessons. When hiring a developer, it is important for them to be transparent and have your best interests at heart and that using shared hosting environments are dangerous.

While my wife and I do not have children yet, we often hear of friends whose children go to school or daycare and come home sick. A shared hosting environment is like a classroom of twenty students. It only takes one sick child to infect the entire classroom.

As you are looking for web hosting, strongly consider a private server or a VPS and if you choose the private server route, make sure that whoever is managing it keeps up with the security and updates associated to that system.

Moving on to the third question, "Does your company host through another provider? If so what is their security policy regarding our data."

Many companies will tell you that they provide hosting, but often they resell a hosting server from another provider. This is a common practice, but it raises a few questions.

The main question is, what is your hosting provider's security policy and service level agreement? From asking the other questions, we know the web developers security policy, but we do not know the policy and guarantees from their hosting provider. We want to ensure that the hosting provider that the web developer uses and resells follows the same security policies and expectations that you have for your business.

The secondary question, which is just as important is "Who manages the server, the third party host or the web developer?" In most cases, the web developer will maintain the private server or employ a third party host to do so. If the third party manages the site, you want to ensure that their update policies are in line with the expectations of your business and the developer.

A company using a third party provider for hosting is a common practice and is not an issue as long as they meet all of the criteria outlined here.

I do not think that it is a bad practice to also know who the third party hosting provider is. This increases transparency.

The final question to ask from the chart in figure 4c is to find out if the company maintains backups of your data. Sometimes this is a service that is extra or bundled into your agreement. It is important to know, in black and white, if you are getting backup service. If you are not getting backups, the next thing to determine is how you can. Not having backups of your site is like not having insurance on your car. You are just asking for trouble.

SERVICE LEVEL AGREEMENT AND UPDATES

The third question in Figure 1a and 1b refers to what the companies' security policies are, service level agreements, and frequency of updates. Much of this was answered in the previous section on web hosting, but it is worth repeating some of this since it is so critical.

The hosting company should be able to provide you with a service level agreement. This outlines the services provided, certain guarantees they provide, and what is expected from each party.

The key component that should be established in this agreement is the exact services that are being provided to you. Some elements to look for are the answers to some of the above questions in terms of how your site is being hosted, how frequently updates are being performed, and who is responsible for carrying out each task. For example, a service level agreement (SLA) may state that they are providing you with a virtual private server with 1TB of transfer per month, with x amount of processing power, and an x amount of storage.

It should provide you with some level of their security procedures, steps that are taken in the event of a data breach, and what amount of uptime they guarantee.

Many hosting providers like Microsoft include in their SLA that they have a financially backed 99.9% uptime guarantee that also includes the latest updates and versions for their hosted software.

I have seen agreements before that state that the hosting company is not liable for acts of God, power grid failures, and other items that are outside of their control. Similar language should be in a strong and honest SLA.

For the core value of data security that we hope to reach through, a component you will want to be very sure of is who is performing the updates and who is responsible to maintain the server. In some situations you may be required to maintain the server and, in others, they may be responsible. Either way is fine, but knowing who is responsible for these items is crucial.

Additionally, an SLA will often refer to measures to remedy breach of the agreement and in what territory legal proceedings are set to occur. This is something that you would hope would never happen, but having it in writing is also vital and key to a good SLA.

Remember these three keys to maintaining a secure web site and web server:

1. Update Frequently
2. Be Proactive in Monitoring
3. Have a Backup that is Secure

In my opinion, it is not unreasonable to tie your web host and website in as part of your quarterly security audit. It increases transparency, awareness, and proactivity that is very important in today's age of frequent data breaches.

CONTENT CHANGES AND ACCESS

An important consideration in hiring a web developer is who has access to make content changes and who has access to the website.

For most organizations, you will want to be able to have control over posting content updates, news posts, and changing verbiage on the site without having to pay the developer to do so.

With a custom developed solution, you may have to submit updates to the web developer. This is okay as long as it aligns with the strategic goals of your company.

As part of your quarterly security audit, you should evaluate who has access. This is important for two reasons. If a third party or the developer has access to the site, you want to know who they are and ensure that their security policies match yours. After development, many web developers keep a login to your website. This is okay and recommended if they are expected to maintain updates, but knowing who they are and what their role in your site management is crucial.

The second thing to consider is internal access. Who on your staff has access to make modifications? Have they been properly trained? Are there persons who had access, but have since left your organization?

When an employee leaves an organization, they are removed from accessing the company files, server, email, and other materials, but website access is often missed. Businesses live and die by documentation. Below, in Figure 4d, is what should be included in a site access chart. Follow this figure in your quarterly audits to know who has access, their role, and if that person has been trained and signed off on your security policy. Figure 4d shows four users who have access to ABC Consulting's website.

Figure 4d. Website Access Chart for ABC Consulting
Name:　Jacob Doe **User ID:**　jdoe **Company:** XYZ Web Solutions **Role:** Maintain Updates and Site Support **Training Status:**　N/A **Security Policy:** Signed 8/01/2014 **Account Active:** Yes
Name:　Regina Black **User ID:**　rblack **Company:** ABC Consulting **Role:** Blog Posting and General Content Updates **Training Status:**　Completed 6/04/2015 **Security Policy:** Signed 6/04/2015 **Account Active:** Yes
Continued on Next Page

Name:	Derrek Emerson
User ID:	demerson
Company:	ABC Consulting
Role:	Internal SEO Management
Training Status:	Completed 07/12/2015
Security Policy:	Signed 07/12/2015
Account Active:	Yes

Maintaining an access and role chart provides business managers with the knowledge of what each person's role is and what element of the site they are accountable for.

This also provides a strong measure for checks and balances to make sure that this listing matches the logins for your site.

Additionally, this chart provides a measure to follow up in the case of an issue with accountability to be able to, 1) know the users role, 2) know the dates of training and security policy acceptance, and 3) determine which members should have access removed.

3ᴿᴰ PARTY ACCESS TO THE WEBSITE

The last question that we posed in Figures 4a and 4b related to the developer keeping a login on the site. We know that the developer having access to the site is okay if they meet our security guidelines. And, in the case of performing updates, it is necessary. We also know that, by using the user access chart in figure 4d, we can maintain a list of the individuals who have access.

This question is more of one for transparency than one that makes or breaks a potential deal.

If a developer does not maintain updates or provide content support then they do not need access and should release the login to you.. If they do still have a role, document it in your website access chart and make sure that their password policies match yours.

REVIEW

Out of necessity, this chapter was a lengthy one. This is an area that most businesses miss when establishing security policies. This is also an area that provides resources for a majority of data breaches. Having a handle on this will strongly enhance your businesses data security and uphold it as a core business value.

CHAPTER 5

DEVICE MANAGEMENT

You may remember the old public service announcement that asked, "It's 10 o'clock. Do you know where your children are?" Hopefully you knew where your children were and if you did not, it would've been emblematic of a larger problem. The reason I reference this commercial is that our children are very important to us and we should know where they are, but do you know where your devices with your crucial data is? At our quarterly security audits we should ask where exactly our company's devices are.

As a test, take out a piece of paper and write down all of your company's hardware devices and where they are located.

Ok, so you have completed your list. Do you have every laptop listed with its location, every flash drive with company data, every machine that has been decommissioned, every company issued cell phone, and every appliance with company data?

Many business managers and technology directors forget about laptops, flash drives, and other materials that employees take home. In the next chapter, we go over data access management, but it is important that you know on which employee-owned devices have company data?

This can be a very lengthy list when you think about this. Every device that has company email should also be included. They all contain YOUR business data and you need to know what devices have it.

Following these measures can prevent accidental internal data breaches and also ensure that the company knows where its assets are located.

In the Office of Personnel Management or OPM breach, they failed to properly document what devices they had, where they were and who had access to them. As stated before, we live and die by the documentation that we have. In programming practices, the first three rules are:

1. Document your work.
2. Document some more.
3. Document it again.

If you do not have such a list, what happens if an employee is terminated or un-expectantly leaves for any reason?

If you are unaware that they have email on a personal device, how do you prevent them from contacting your business clients or vendors?

This is a very complicated issue that can be easily resolved with good documentation.

Acme Medical Corporation had an issue with employees taking data outside of the organization to another organization to complete work. In some instances, this may be okay, but for Acme Medical Corporation, HIPPA required the documents to be completed onsite. By not being aware of a portable data device being used to store patient information, HIPPA was breached, creating an issue for Acme Medical Corporation.

For many businesses and organizations the use of USB flash drives is important for staff to work remotely if the company does not have virtual desktops or cloud storage. In the age of the cloud, I prefer to see our clients ban external storage devices and use cloud storage from a provider that facilitates a remote deletion of the files. This way, your business is in full control of access to data.

If your company's staff utilizes external storage, be cautious. It is hard to know for sure what data an employee has on their personal storage device. If you choose to allow external storage, have company-issued storage devices/USB drives and enact the policy in Figure 5a.

Figure 5a. Use of Removable Storage Devices
*ABC Consulting understands that to allow our employees to have flexibility in their work that they need to have removable storage devices to transport company data. To achieve our core value of data security, we allow this **only** through company issued storage device. New hires will be issued a company owned portable storage device and existing staff may request them. You are not permitted to use a personally owned storage device or to transfer company data to any machine outside of company control. Doing so is a violation of our security policy, which may result in termination. Upon termination or resignation the company owned storage device is to be returned. Not doing so may require legal action. If prior to this policies implementation on this date, you have used a personal device to store company data you have 14 days to remove the data and notify management that the data has been removed.*

Portable storage devices are very cheap and, if your staff needs to use them so to prevent business from being impacted, implement this policy and provide company-owned flash drives/removable storage.

In the mobile society that we thrive in, most businesses provide employee email and other services that are accessed on personal devices owned by the employee. This is important to ensure fast communication and accessibility for your staff, but it also provides a possibility for a data breach. Larger companies may be able to issue company phones and tablets for use that they can control, but many companies cannot afford this. To protect your business and know what devices have access to your data, consider utilizing the policy for ABC Consulting on mobile devices in Figure 5b.

Figure 5b. ABC Consulting Mobile Device Policy

ABC Consulting is aware of the need for rapid access to email and other information. To allow employees to have access, but maintain data security we have established the following policy as part of our organizations core value of data security. Employees are permitted to have access to company email, calendar, and contact information on their personal devices providing that the following takes place.

1) *Employees follow the companies password policy for their personal devices and company email*
2) *Employees register each of their devices, that access company data, with the companies technology coordinator*
3) *Upon termination or resignation, the technology coordinator must be provided with the registered devices for safe removal of company data*
4) *At any time this privilege can be revoked if the employee fails to meet criteria outlined in the security policy*
5) *If an employee owned device becomes infected with any virus/malware or other form of malicious software, they must notify the technology director immediately and let them resolve the issue and review the possibility for a data breach. Employees will not be punished for complying with this policy and only for non-compliance risk the possibility for termination or other legal action*

It should also be noted that failure to register a device with the company could result in termination or other action. We encourage usage of mobile devices and also transparency.

Figure 5b does a few things. It makes the employees accountable for their device and allows you to know where data is stored. Additionally, it does not punish an employee who accidentally has a device become compromised if they are transparent and honest.

This policy is designed to provide the capacity for them to have access, but also protect the company and its goals for data security.

Establishing a good list of devices that have company data is very important and can be time consuming, but by enacting these measures, it facilitates a much easier catalog of devices that the company does not have direct control over.

Now let's go back to the list you drafted. If you have every single piece of hardware on your list and feel it is complete, I encourage you to follow up and ask around the office to see if the list is complete or if you are missing some devices. Chances are, you do not know which employees have email on their mobile devices or what external devices have your data on them. This is normal, but it is of utmost importance to regain control of your assets. In Figure 5c, you can see an outline for the type of data you should have in your list.

Figure 5c. Device Management Data
What is the hardware? Does the company own it? Who is responsible for the data it contains? Where is the device located? Was the device approved by technology coordinator? Who has access to the device? Was it accounted for in the last quarterly security audit? Is the device still in use or has it been decommissioned? When is the device scheduled for decommission?

In Figure 5c, we mention decommissioning of devices. What this refers to is a device that has reached the end of its useful life and no longer receives updates from the manufacturer. When this time occurs, the company should either internally destroy the device or hire an outside firm to handle its removal and decommissioning. For cell phones, useful life ends typically every two years, but this figure is increasing. For PCs and servers, their useful life is normally every five years. Knowing what devices fall out of support is critical in protecting your data. If an outside firm handles the decommission of a device, you will want them to provide you with a document stating that the data has been removed or properly destroyed, and in that document, list the identifying information for that hardware.

This protects the company in the circumstance where the organization decommissioning does not fulfill their requirement and holds them accountable for the data that they were to destroy. A similar document should also be created internally for internal decommissioning of hardware. In the technological age we live in, devices quickly become outdated, and having procedures in place to handle their removal is more than necessary. Businesses can ensure that all hardware with company access are documented by running a scan on the network. While this will not account for removable devices, it will account for all devices that are connected to your company's network. There are many companies that provide this type of scan, but a free utility you can use if you have the staff to properly interpret its findings, is AngryIP. You can download this tool at http://angryip.org/download/.

If used properly, this will report all of the devices connected to your company's network. If you missed a device in your audit, this is a good way of making sure that the device finds its way to your list.

As you craft your device list, make sure that it includes the following:

- Firewalls
- Servers both Internal and External
- Network appliances such as switches and backups
- Company-owned workstations, laptops, tablets, cell phones and removable storage
- Employee-owned laptops, mobile devices, and removable storage devices
- Company scanners, copiers, and printers
- Other company-owned resources that contain data

CHAPTER 6

DATA ACCESS MANAGEMENT

This chapter pulls the last five together. Up to this point, all of the items we have discussed have been related to data access and management of those who have access. In chapter one, we took a look at the hardware and software 'walls' that barricade ourselves from the outside (when used properly) from accessing our business data. Chapter two, we started to look at regulating passwords to ensure data access security and minimize risks of password compromise. In the third chapter, we then covered software updates and learned that vulnerable software often provides hackers a back door in accessing your data or system resources. Remember we referenced the Flash hack that affected users who went to Yahoo websites that were loaded with ads containing malware.

These three chapters provided a good backbone to establish a core value in data security. In chapters four and five, we took a look at website access, device access, and other components that internal staff or third party developers have access to and the potential areas for breaches.

This is a very hands-on chapter. In the last chapter, we reviewed devices that contain your data, but now we are going to look at it from a user level. Some of this may be a repeat, but that's ok as we are auditing all of the access points.

First, let's take a look at external sources that have access to your data. While many companies may host aspects of your business and not have direct access to the data, some may have direct access. In Figure 6a (below), we take a look at ABC Consulting's external access chart.

Figure 6a. External Access Chart for ABC Consulting		
Company	User	Role/Access Level
XYZ Web Develop.	James F.	1)Site Updates 2)Access to Website Data
	Frank B.	1)Site Email List 2)Access to Site Data
Computer Tech Firm	Gaven E.	1) Internal Admin Access 2) Manage Systems, Servers, and Workstations 3) Admin Access to Email Server
	Ken B.	1)Internal Admin Access 2) Resolve Service Requests
Printing Solutions LLC	Janelle C.	1) Internal Admin Access 2) Install and Manage Print/Scan Devices
Management Software	Nate B.	1)Admin access to manage our outsourced cloud management server
Microsoft	No Specific User	Role and Access Implemented Temporarily Upon Request

In the above figure you can see an example of their external access audit. I encourage you to recreate your own list using a spreadsheet tool like Excel and add other fields, such as date they signed the security policy if applicable, and if they are currently active in the system.

Logging companies that once had access, but you no longer work with is also important if you previously had a breach but were not aware. An example of this is in Figure 6b.

Figure 6a. Former External Access Chart		
Company	User	Role/Access Level
High Tech Managers	Bob P.	Former Managed Services Provider Access Revoked 4/02/2012 and verified by Computer Tech Firm

Many small businesses like ABC Consulting outsource their technology management, print services, and email providers. In this chart, you can see that they have a site developed by XYZ Web Development, the users, and what the users have access to. We can also see that they employ a computer tech firm to manage their network, email server, and handle service requests. The access level for those users are also noted. Along with the tech firm managing their email system, they also have email support from Microsoft, with no specific user and access provided.

You can also see that they have company Management Software that manages their cloud-based company management system. Many companies have this. There are a lot of great cloud based software suites out there that help streamline your business. Noting them is important as well, even though they may only use your system when you request support. Many data breaches are through third party providers. Knowing who they are and checking in on them to ensure they meet your security policy is important and puts the liability for breaches on them.

Knowledge is power and proper documentation of who has access is important, especially if your business is small.. You should review your new security policies with outside companies that have access to your data and request that they sign off on the policy. This is more important for managed service providers, web developers, and print service providers that are small and local. Larger companies like Microsoft, IBM, and others already have security policies in place, but reviewing your policies with your direct contact with those firms is important as well.

An important side note to this book is that, if you work with a Technology Consultant or Managed Services Provider, rather than having in-house personnel, you should work with them as you implement these policies to make sure that you are achieving your core value of data security. Please note that they may charge you for this service depending on your support agreement, but it is a cost that should be highly considered as you review, enact, and move forward.

Now that we have analyzed external data access, we now need to assess internal data access. Depending on the size of your company, this can be a much longer task.

To get started, take out a piece of paper or open an Excel file and make a list of all of your company's current employees.

Often times, when I ask users to do this, we find that their list is much shorter than the list of users in their directory. At

Solinkit, we specialize with Microsoft and IBM Lotus systems. Your system may vary, but take your list to the person who manages that authentication system for your network and have them match up your list with the list in the server for both email, file access, and domain login.

For any name not on the list, have the technology provider fill out a form similar to the one in Figure 6c.

Figure 6c. Unreported User Access
Name: Derek White
User ID: dwhite
Department: Accounting
Last Access Date: 06/14/2015
Date of Audit: 08/11/2015
Printer Access: Yes
Email Access: No
Network Access: Yes
File Access: Yes
Name: Sandy Sue
User ID: ssue
Department: Support Staff
Last Access Date: 08/10/2015
Date of Audit: 08/11/2015
Printer Access: Yes
Email Access: Yes
Network Access: Yes
File Access: Yes

In Figure 6c, we had two users that were reported that were not on our list for ABC Consulting. It is your job to evaluate the users that have access and determine if they were missed or if they should have been revoked. In this instance, the first user, Derek White, had resigned in June and his email access removed by the technology coordinator. His internal login access to the network though was still active. The last access date in this is important because it lets us know that, even though Derek still had access, he did not log into company resources.

For this user you should create and submit a form similar to Figure 6d to your technology provider.

Figure 6c. User Removal Request
Name: Derek White
User ID: dwhite
Nature of the Request: This user resigned on 06/14/2015. Immediately remove all access from this user and disable all of their accounts. Please notify upon completion

You can be as detailed with your user update requests as you want. I would prefer there be more information than we use in Figure 6c because it established a strong paper trail to refer back to if an issue would ever arise.

Sandy Sue was a new hire that you did not list, but does need access to the system. Inform your technology coordinator and add her into your list.

So far, we have established a list of internal users that have access to the site, audited users who have access, removed who needed removed, and added users to the list that we missed. Now it is time to go more in-depth into our user access list.

CHAPTER 7

EMAIL SECURITY & POLICY

While writing this book, I am being constantly provided with several great points of reference involving email security in the workplace. When you think about email security, it is on a much larger scale than just being careful with not opening attachments. In chapter five, we discussed device management and which devices have access to your data. Now with the recent hack of Ashley Madison, I have additional points to include.

For those of you that are unaware, Ashley Madison is a site that promises discrete affairs for married people. A group of hackers exploited their database and posted between 30-40 million email address of the users online. Of course this hack is emblematic of a larger problem with our society, but I mention this hack because the vast majority of the users signed up for their accounts using a company email address.

Email addresses for the United Nations, Bank of America, IBM, Harvard, Yale, Vatican, Amazon, and many others were used to register for the service. This is the perfect storm for a data breach at the business level. A user signs up and uses their company email address and the same password they use at work. Hackers get this data and bingo access to even more data.

Hillary Clinton has also been in hot water relating to this topic of email security. Clinton allegedly used a personal email server and received Top Secret content. Where many Ashley Madison used their work email for too many outside things, it seems that Mrs. Clinton may have attempted to bypass her government-issued email address. All of these topics fall into the topic of email security and all can be addressed with a strong email security policy. One thing a policy won't do is prevent people who deliberately have the intention of going against the policy, however the policy should be put into place to protect the business from liability and put together procedures for an employee that violates the policy.

STARTING TO FORM AN EMAIL POLICY

Creating any formal policy can be a challenge. It is important to explain why the policy is important and be clear in what you establish. A good Email Policy should include the following:

1. Overview
2. Purpose
3. Scope
4. Policy
5. Policy Compliance
6. Revision History

To get started, let's take a look at the overview aspect of the policy. In your overview, you should discuss why the policy is important.

The SANS Institute has some great examples of Email Policy plans. In their overview in a document published in 2013, they listed the following:

Electronic email is pervasively used in almost all industry verticals and is often the primary form of communication and awareness method within an organization. At the same time, misuse of email can post many legal, privacy and security risks, thus it's important for users to understand the appropriate use of electronic communication.

This is a great overview and can be adapted to best fit your organization. What I like about it is that it is a very strong and universal overview to the policy. It addresses the importance of email being used and also the reason for the policy from a business standpoint. It sets the tone for the rest of the document and conveys the benefit to the employees. You will always have staff who are resistant to adding policies, but I feel the verbiage in the overview they use is key into setting the tone of protecting the business and the reasons why misuse can produce harm.

The next item in putting together the policy is addressing the specific purpose of the policy. A good example used by ABC Consulting is the following:

The purpose of this email policy is to ensure the proper use of ABC Consulting's email system and make users aware of what ABC Consulting deems as acceptable and unacceptable use of its email system. This policy outlines the minimum requirements for use of email controlled within ABC Consulting.

This is a clear statement and outlines the purpose of the policy. It also provides the context for the rest of the document, when we get into defining specific policies.

Now that we have both the overview of the policy and the purpose we need to define the scope or the reach of the policy. Defining a scope is important to ensure that everyone who reads the policy understands and to what it applies. Using the template from the SANS Institute, ABC Consulting was able to put together a strong scope.

This policy covers appropriate use of any email send from an ABC Consulting email address and applies to all employees, vendors, and agents operating on behalf of ABC Consulting.

OUTLINING SPECIFIC POLICIES

As we outline the policies below, some are standard from the SANS Institute and others are ones that I feel need to be added to keep current with the mobile and web-driven society in which we live. The policies below were drafted for our example firm, ABC Consulting.

Policy 1: All use of email must be consistent with ABC Consulting's policies and procedures of ethical conduct, safety, compliance with applicable laws and proper business practices.

This first policy is very generic and may require some clarification. Having a good human resources policy for what the company's procedures of ethical conduct are is essential. Some of these items are addressed in the Acceptable Use Policy we discuss in Chapter 8. This prevents any confusion on what the expectation is for employee behavior. The issue of safety and compliance is outlined more in Chapter 10 as we develop the Security Policy.

Policy 2: ABC Consulting's email accounts should be used primarily for ABC Consulting's business related purposes personal communication is permitted on a limited basis, but non-ABC Consulting related communication related to commercial uses is prohibited.

This second policy addresses the expected use for company email and establishes that other commercial use with the email address for the company is prohibited. The language in this policy does allow limited personal use. You may decide to completely prohibit personal use, but that depends mostly on the nature of your company. When I think of limited personal use, my thought is occasional emails to my wife to coordinate our schedules and other items of that nature. As you establish these policies you should educate your staff on your company's interpretation of limited personal use. I think that completely banning some personal emails may be counter intuitive and cause employees to access their personal email during work..

Policy 3: All ABC Consulting data contained within an email message or an attachment must be secured according to the Data Protection Standards.

This policy outlines the expectation of the level of security for outgoing email. Depending on the industry, your organization may have stricter Data Protection Standards. Organizations working with sensitive materials such as tax documents, patient information, and legal services will have a stronger Data Protection Standard that requires encryption and other measures. Smaller organizations may simply require that you verify the message is being sent to a person authorized to view it. Many organizations require a disclaimer on emails that establishes whether an email can be distributed and shared. For further information on this research specific requirements to your industry and talk with your legal counsel on what your industry requirements should be.

Policy 4: Email should only be retained if it qualifies as an ABC Consulting business record. Email is an ABC Consulting business record if there exists a legitimate and ongoing business reason to preserve the information contained in the email.

This policy addresses clutter in the email system as well requiring business records that have a reason to be stored, filed in a folder. Having emails from past clients (if not legally required to maintain them, which we talk about in Policy 5) is data that can be protected by removing it. Some industries have requirements on how long email should be stored. When that time is up, old emails should be deleted. This allows you to not only establish data security, but also remove unneeded data. If you no longer have a reason to store the message, then it is a waste of funds to spend securing it. We live in a world where most people don't delete anything. With all of this information being stored, a data breach can be even more damaging.

Policy 5: Email that is identified as an ABC Consulting business record shall be retained according to the ABC Consulting Record Retention Schedule.

This policy addresses how long business records are stored. Various industries have varying requirements on the amount of time that data must be retained. In Figure 7a, we can see regulatory minimums that impact many businesses.

Figure 7a Data Retention Minimums	
Internal Revenue Service	7 Years
Payment Card or PCI	1 Year
California Franchise Tax Board	4 Years
DISA Security Technical Guides	1 Year
Average State Revenue Departments	3 Years
HIPPA Section 164	6 Years

Policy 6: The ABC Consulting email system shall not be used for the creation or distribution of any disruptive or offensive messages, including offensive comments about race, gender, hair color, disabilities, age, sexual orientation, pornography, religious beliefs and practice, political beliefs, or national origin. Employees who receive any emails with this content from any other employee should report the matter to their supervisor immediately.

Policy 6 is pretty self-explanatory. If you are going to email someone something that you wouldn't say in front of the company's human resource rep, don't send it.

Policy 7: Users are prohibited from automatically forwarding ABC Consulting email to a third party email system. Individual messages which are forwarded by the user must not contain ABC Consulting confidential or other information.

This is important. While we can lock an employee out of emails when they leave the company, without this policy, they could still have access to vital company data in a personal email outside of the company's control. Keep in mind the current incident with Hillary Clinton having messages go to her private server containing alleged Top Secret information. This policy sets the precedent that company emails stay on the company's email system.

Policy 8: Users are prohibited from using third-party email systems and storage servers such as Google, Yahoo, Hotmail, and others to conduct ABC Consulting business, to create or memorialize any binding transactions, or to store or retain email on behalf of ABC Consulting. Such communications and transactions are prohibited by default and must be approved through proper channels and documentation.

This policy further establishes expectations for personal email and storage accounts, ensuring that company data stays within company control.

Policy 9: Using a reasonable amount of ABC Consulting resources for personal emails is acceptable, but non-work related email shall be saved in a separate folder from word related email.

This policy builds from policy 2. If you are going to send limited personal emails using the company account, those emails must be filed separately in a folder that does not contain word data.

Policy 10: ABC Consulting employees shall have no expectation of privacy in anything they store, send or receive on the company's email system. Further, ABC Consulting may monitor messages without notice.

Policy 10 establishes compliance with the above policies and sets the tone that the company owns the email system and has the right to monitor it or review emails in an audit or as part of compliance management.

Policy 11: ABC Consulting employees should only sign up for online services that are directly required for their work related tasks. Using ABC Consulting issued email to sign up for non-work related online services is strictly prohibited.

This policy is an addition that I feel is necessary given the current breach from Ashley Madison. No matter your feelings on the online affair service, one thing is for sure and that's employees shouldn't have used their company emails for the service. In addition, this policy should prevent employees from using company email for signing up for Facebook, Pandora, Amazon, eBay, and other services that are not necessary for their work.

COMPLIANCE WITH THE POLICY

Now that we have our policies listed, ensuring compliance is the next item that we need to address. As part of the compliance procedures, we have compliance measurement, exceptions, and steps that take place for non-compliance.

To ensure compliance, your company should verify compliance through a variety of audits and feedback from management. Depending on the size of your organization, you may want to hire an external firm to periodically come in to verify that employees are following the policy. It is important that the entire company understand that if they need an exception to this policy for any reason that they must get approval from the management team and technology coordinator in writing.

It is important in your compliance portion of your policy to outline what actions may take place for an employee who violates the policy. A good example of a non-compliance procedure for ABC Consulting is below.

An employee found to have violated this policy may be subject to disciplinary action, up to and including termination of employment.

When you take a firm stance that includes the possibility of termination, you have educated your employees about following policy. Failure to educate the staff on the policies is a failure on the management level and not the employee level.

REVISION HISTORY

One good thing to do with any policy is establishing a revision history. This allows tracking of policy revisions. Figure 7b shows an example of a revision history table.

Figure 7b. Revision History Table		
Date	Responsible	Summary of Change
July 10, 2015	Human Resources	Added Policy 11

CHAPTER 8

ACCEPTABLE USE POLICY

An acceptable use policy is also important for outlining what is viewed as acceptable behavior by employees.

You may wonder why this policy fits into a book on data security. Preventing malware and vulnerabilities inside of your network is crucial to protecting your company's core value of data security. Establishing a good policy to address the human element of use will build upon the layers we talked about in the earlier chapter. Deliberate employee action can often times result in a data breach.

Like the Email Policy, the Acceptable Use policy has several similar categories.

1. Overview
2. Purpose
3. Scope
4. Policy
   a. General Use
   b. Security and Sensitive Information
   c. Unacceptable Use
5. Policy Compliance
6. Revision History

FORMING THE ACCEPTABLE USE POLICY

Overview

In this overview it is important to explain that the policy is not intended to impose restrictions on staff, but rather to protect the employees and other company affiliates. Below is an example outline for ABC Consulting.

The intentions for publishing this Acceptable Use Policy is not to impose restrictions that are contrary to ABC Consulting's established culture of openness, trust and integrity. ABC Consulting is committed to protecting their employees, partners, and the company from illegal or damaging actions by individuals either knowingly or unknowingly. Company systems are to be used for business purposes in serving the interested of the company, and of our clients and customers in the course of normal operations.

A strong core value of data security is a team effort involving the full participation and support of all employees and affiliates that deal with our information systems. It is vital for every computer user to know these guidelines, and conduct their activities accordingly.

Purpose

With any document it is important for it to have a purpose that is clear and concise. Its purpose is to explain the reason the policy is important and why it must be in place. This is very important as it outlines why the policy is important to the company's core value of data security.

The purpose of this policy is to outline the acceptable use of the company's electronic equipment at ABC Consulting. These policies are in place to protect the employee and company. Inappropriate use exposes ABC Consulting to the risks including virus attacks, malware, compromised data security, and legal issues.

Scope

It is important to be clear in the scope to say that if employees use personal devices to connect to company data, that they apply to this policy as well.

The policy applies to the use for all information, electronic devices, and network resources to conduct ABC Consulting business and interact with business systems provided by ABC consulting. This policy applies to any device connected to any company resources, including but not limited to personal electronics connected to company provided email or file storage. All employees, contractors, and affiliates are responsible for utilizing good judgement regarding appropriate use of information, electronic, devices, and other resources. This policy applies to employees, contractors, and other workers at ABC Consulting, including all personnel affiliated with third parties. This policy applies to all devices that contain company data.

GENERAL USE POLICIES

This section of the policy covers general usage on the network and covers the main ownership of company data and system usage.

Policy 1: ABC Consulting proprietary information stored on any electronic device whether owned by ABC Consulting, the employee, or a third party remains the property of ABC Consulting. You must ensure through all means that proprietary information is protected in accordance with our standard as it relates to our core value of security.

Policy 2: Employees have the responsibility to promptly report theft, loss, or unauthorized disclosure of proprietary information.

Policy 3: You may access, use or share ABC Consulting information only to the extent of fulfilling your assigned job duties.

Policy 4: Employees are responsible for exercising good judgement regarding the reasonableness of personal use. Individual departments may have specific guidelines regarding usage.

Policy 5: For security and network maintenance, authorized individuals within ABC Consulting may monitor equipment and systems at any time.

SECURITY POLICIES

This section of the Acceptable Use Policy addresses general security policies that employees should utilize on a daily basis. Much of the information outlined here was elaborated in more detail in both Chapter 2 (Secure Passwords) and Chapter 5 (Device Management).

Policy 1: All mobile and computing devices that connect to the company's network or resources must comply with ABC Consulting's guidelines for Device and Data Access Management, along with our Password Policy.

Policy 2: User passwords must comply with the Password Policy and providing access to another individual, either deliberately or through failure to secure access is prohibited.

Policy 3: All devices must be secured with a password-protected screensaver with the auto lock feature enabled. You must lock or log off your machine when the device is unattended.

Policy 4: Employees must use extreme caution when opening email attachments received either un-expectantly or from unknown senders. These attachments may contain malware that could compromise our organizations data.

UNACCEPTABLE USE

Now that we have outlined the general usage and policies for system security, we now need to review what is unacceptable. There are many items that can be added in addition to my list here, but this provides a good foundation to build upon.

Policy 1: Under no circumstances is an employee of ABC Consulting authorized to engage in any activity that is illegal under local, state, federal or international law while utilizing company owned resources.

Policy 2: The following network related activities are strictly prohibited, with absolutely no exceptions:

1) *Violations of the rights of any person or company protected by copyright, trade secret, patent or other intellectual property, or similar laws or regulations, including, but not limited to, the installation or distribution of "pirated" or other software products that are not licensed for use by ABC Consulting.*
2) *Unauthorized copying of copyrighted materials and the installation of any copyrighted software for which ABC Consulting does not have an active license is strictly prohibited.*

3) Accessing data for any purpose other than conducting business, even if you have authorized access is prohibited.
4) Introduction of malicious programs into the network, including, but not limited to viruses, worms, Trojan horses, e-mail bombs, etc.
5) Revealing your account passwords to others or allowing the use of your account by others.
6) Using ABC Consulting resources to actively engage in procuring or transmitting material that is in violation of sexual harassment laws.
7) Making fraudulent claims for products or services originating from any ABC Consulting account.
8) Port scanning, network monitoring, or security scanning is expressly prohibited, unless part of our quarterly security audit and conducted by authorized personnel.
9) Conducting Denial of Service Attacks and/or interfering with business operation services.
10) Providing information about, or lists of ABC Consulting employees or parties outside of ABC Consulting.

Policy 3: Email Communication and Activities

1) Employees should not send unsolicited email messages, including the sending of junk mail.
2) Employees are prohibited from sending any email that may be considered harassing in nature.
3) Forging email header information is strictly prohibited.
4) Crating or forwarding chain letters are strictly prohibited.
5) For additional details please consult the Email Security Policy

Policy 4: Blogging and Social Media Expectations

1) *Blogging or posting on social media by employees even on personal computer systems is subject to the terms and restrictions set forth in this policy. Posting may not be detrimental to ABC Consulting's best interests, and does not interfere with an employee's regular work duties. Use of social media or blogging platforms on ABC Consulting's system is subject to monitoring.*

2) *Employees are prohibited from revealing any confidential or proprietary information, trade secrets or any other material considered confidential.*

3) *Employees cannot attribute personal statements, opinions or beliefs to ABC Consulting when engaged in social media, blogs, and forums.*

COMPLIANCE FOR ACCEPTABLE USE POLICY

Much like the Email Security Policy, the compliance for the Acceptable Use Policy should be monitored by the company's security committee, management, and technology coordinator. This can be completed through various methods including, but not limited to, business tool reports, audits conducted internally and externally, and feedback from the employees and policy owner.

It is important to educate the staff so they have the knowledge they need to be successful in following the policy. Employees found in violation should be subject to disciplinary action and possible termination.

REVISION HISTORY

As stated in Chapter 8, a good table tracking Revision History is good for maintaining a log of the policies modifications. Figure 8a recaps this table for us to use as we revise the policies.

7b. Revision History Table		
Date	**Responsible**	**Summary of Change**
April 25, 2015	Human Resources	Added Policy 4

REVIEW

Chapter 7 and 8 may have been lengthy, but it is vital to establishing the core value of data security. There are many additional levels and additional policies that you may wish to utilize, but these two chapters should provide a good start at putting together the procedures required to maintain a good foundation of security. Please note that before enacting these policies, you should work with your legal team and human resource manager to ensure that the policies meet the standards that you need in order to achieve your goals.

Chapter 9

Clean Desk Rule

It is surprising the amount of threats that businesses encounter that happen through non-technical means. One major non-technical threat is easily preventable by following the clean desk rule.

My desk is certainly not clean, but it does comply with the clean desk rule that I am going to talk about. Right now, if a competitor was to be sitting at my desk, they would find my workstation locked and no sensitive files on my desk. They may find some receipts for restaurants I have visited, an old cup of coffee, and some empty soda cans, but not much else.

What is on your desk right now? Is your computer locked and are sensitive files put away? Do you have stacks of paper on your desk that you need to review?

Who is your biggest competitor? If they were at your desk would they find anything useful? It is important to remember that anyone can see what is on your desk, especially in a cubical environment. Keeping your desk clear of critical information is vital to establishing good security. You never know who may come across your desk to drop something off and see something that they are not supposed to see.

A year or so we had a client that had an issue with one of their employees downloading pirated materials. Upon interviewing the individual and their management team, we determined that there was no possible way that they could have been the culprit as they were out on vacation during the time of the violation. As members of my team worked to clean up the machine and remove the malware and pirated files, I walked into the office and asked him how he logged in since I had the password for the workstation. He pointed to a sticky note on the monitor. Bingo!

At this moment it was clear what had happened. While the employee was out, another employee had used his workstation under the other employee's credentials.

Treat your password like your Social Security number. If you wouldn't put that open on your desk or in plain view, treat your password with the same respect.

The clean desk policy is more than just not leaving passwords in the open, but also about leaving sensitive information laying around.

This policy can be very hard to follow, especially for managers and executives that are very busy with full workloads, but it truly is essential to protecting your business.

This same principle should be applied to the use of printers as well. Once there was a company that we consulted for and the accountant mistakenly sent a print off of staff salaries to the community printer instead of their private unit in their office. While this was a mistake, it generated a series of issues since staff that should not have seen the information, now had access to it.

If you are going to print something that is sensitive, ensure that you are the first to get it or request a personal printer. If you have a series of documents on your desk for review, get a filing cabinet with a folder specifically for those documents. When you leave your desk you need to be 100% certain that if for whatever reason another person is at your desk, that there is no information laying around that you wouldn't have otherwise provided to them.

This is important and should be yet another item you should add to your security policy or implement into your acceptable use policy for company data.

CHAPTER 10

STAFF EDUCATION

Now that we have a good fundamental understanding of the technology, documentation, policy and other requirements to establish a strong data security core value, we need to work to convey that message to our employees.

As frequently as new threats emerge, my thought is that a quarterly meeting to review and educate staff should be a goal. The reason quarterly meetings fit well into this strategy is because of the quarterly audits that you should be preforming on your company's data security. These meetings should not be long and should have time for open discussion. At first, when introducing these policies, you may want to schedule a half day meeting to cover all of the objectives and values of your strategy. This half day overview of the company's data security policy should be used in one of three scenarios.

1. First implementation of the Policies and Core Value
2. Educating new hires
3. In a circumstance where several staff are not following the policies and procedures

Many business owners and managers may think that this is a lot of time that could be spent on company operations and that the lost labor time is very costly, but a recent study from the Ponemon Institute found that the average data breach currently costs businesses on average an estimated $5.5 million. A combination of the 'walls' we discussed earlier in combination with strong policies, and education is a small

Rather than taking the employees through the process in a professional, you-can-do-it way, the presenter framed it at a big, almost overwhelming deal.

The presenter struggled through navigating the demo due to constant questions from the staff, resulting in multiple tangents. As the demo continued, remarks of frustration from both the presenter and staff filled the meeting and without any useful information being conveyed to the staff, the meeting abruptly ended.

The executives of the company were frustrated because of the poor training. They conveyed the poor training to a poor product. The product that we rolled out was excellent and they are using it to this day.

I always appreciated the way that Jim would stand up for my team.

To the irritated executives, Jim said, "The email system you moved to is greatly efficient and will not only increase productivity, but save your company thousands a year. Reschedule the training for tomorrow at 8:30 and let Nathan give the presentation. They agreed and the next day I trained the staff.

When they all came in and sat down, I could tell that they already had performed negativity about the training and that some damage control was required. I went early and made sure that everyone had what they needed when they entered the conference room. "Do you want a coffee or soda", I asked. "Go get that now while we wait", I told them. When 8:25 rolled around and still had some of their staff missing, I had the secretary send out a call that everyone needed to be in their seats by 8:30 as the training was going to begin.

Once everyone was seated and comfortable, I began my presentation.

I started by telling them to clear their minds and forget everything that occurred the previous day. I then instructed them to all have a moment of silence for 60 seconds to clear their minds. This did two things. Firstly, it broke some of the animosity that I had felt. Secondly it ensured that the room was silent when I began speaking.

I started my presentation with strong posture and a smile. It is hard to recall exactly what I said, but I think it was something like this:

Thank you all for attending. I like to talk and ask that you hold your questions for later, since I may answer them as I move along. Many of you yesterday were told of some big changes. Forget that all for a moment and let's look at where the organization was at last year. The email system that had been in use for almost a decade was antiquated and causing you all a lot of grief with incompatibilities. Additionally, the organization has fallen into some budgetary constraints and paying yearly licenses for an old system does not make sense. What we have done, in collaboration with your executive team, was put together a good five year technology plan that will not only give you the best system that is on the market, but also resolve many problems you had. I have a good feeling that many of you are already familiar with the product and use a similar version at home so let's go forward and take a look at how you will not only save time, but have a better user experience with these changes.

It was clear after this strong introduction that I had not only their attention, but a positive mindset. It's very interesting how entering a meeting with a positive outlook or negative outlook will set the mood for those to whom you are presenting. After the training had ended and I answered their questions, all of their concerns and fears were gone. They moved forward with starting to use the new system and have seen many positive outcomes from the implementation.

Here are some lessons I hope that you learn from this example:

1. Set a firm time to begin the presentation and make attendance mandatory.
2. If the employees need to bring materials with them, let them know the day before.
3. Have some coffee or other refreshments available to make them comfortable.
4. Approach the meeting with positive body language and a positive outlook.
5. Set up an agenda for the orientation and ask that questions be held until the question and answer session.
6. Provide handout materials.
7. Express the importance and positive nature of what your business is trying to achieve through this meeting.

Sorry I got off on a little side story there, but I think it is important to understand. People do not like change and, in your orientation on your new data security policies, you need to be as upbeat and positive as possible. This will set the tone for a very good meeting, training, and/or orientation.

Now it's the day of our orientation on data security policies. We have the policies printed out to distribute, we have a time set, some refreshments are available, and staff are coming in, signing in and ready.

A strong opening statement is very important. If I were presenting a new data security policy today, I might start the orientation with something like this:

We are all aware of the problem that our country has had in recent years, months, and days with data security. Large companies and organizations like Target, Home Depot, Office of Personnel Management, and others have fallen victim to data breaches. Data breaches cost millions of dollars per business every year. At ABC Consulting, we have a high value on protecting our employees, our company, and customers. We think of ourselves as a company that is on the leading edge, fostering creativity, productivity, and an awesome work environment. We want to continue that trend and ensure that we are all secure with our information that we use daily. You all know that we have a strong commitment to transparency, trust, and openness.

Establishing a strong core value of data security is a team effort involving the full participation and support from all of you and I am very excited that we at ABC Consulting can proudly take part in establishing these goals to ensure security at our company. These policies protect all of us and will further our company's vision.

You can open how you would like, but something like this with a positive spin and body language should result in a successful orientation.

Before diving into the policies that directly impact the employees and the measures that they will need to take, spend some time talking about the company's role. I would discuss the 'walls' that we discussed in the first chapter and the measures that the company has taken to protect the employees with firewalls, antivirus, antispam, and other tools that are being utilized to secure the business network. This will convey that it is not a one-sided effort and that the company is doing its part to achieve the target of data security.

After reviewing the company's measures, take a brief moment to answer questions that specifically relate to that aspect of security.

When I was on vacation this year, my wife and I went into a piano bar where they take song suggestions written on napkins. If they received a song that they were planning on doing later, they would hold off on playing it for the time until it fit into their set. You could take this same approach to prevent tangents that can kill a well-structured meeting.

What I would suggest is to take all of the questions before answering them and put them on the whiteboard. Have one section of the board for questions that relate to a certain component of the presentation and another section of the whiteboard for questions that will be answered later.

After the Q&A, it is time to start the next part of the presentation. I would suggest reviewing what we discussed in Chapter 9 in regard to non-technical threats, the clean desk policy and social engineering.

When this is done, take any questions and then provide a 15 minute break. This way when they come back to the orientation, you can dive into the acceptable use policy, email policy, password policy, and others that you have decided to establish.

Slowly go over each and elaborate on why certain policies are being enacted. Your audience will appreciate this because you do not want them to feel like they are being punished, but rather protected.

After the meeting is over, have two piles for the employees to put their signed policy forms. One pile for those that understand the policies and accept them and another for employees that have a few additional questions.

I find it best for those who have a hard time understanding any implementation to speak to them one-on-one. This gives them your direct attention and ensures that all questions are addressed.

If after the orientation and one-on-one sessions, employees that still do not want to agree to the policy may need to be terminated. It may sound harsh, but as you analyze your team and your people, you don't want the others to be affected by one who does not wish to follow your company's new adopted value of data security. It only takes one small hole in a bucket to cause a leak and the same goes to data breaches.

THE QUARTERLY MEETING

Now that we have the orientation process out of the way, our quarterly security review will be much simpler and require less time. An hour or two should be enough for a quarterly security meeting and possibly less depending on the results of your quarterly security audit. This meeting could also be incorporated as a topic in other quarterly meetings that your company has.

This meeting should cover the following:

1. Review of the password policy with a reminder that it is time for passwords to be changed
2. Any issues found in the quarterly audit
3. Any changes that are being made to the policies
4. Any external threats that are currently affecting other organizations that the team needs to be aware
5. Questions or concerns from the staff regarding data security

A reminder is always nice, which is why I think starting the meeting with a reminder to update passwords is a great way to start. It is human nature for us to forget things and a reminder is a helpful way to make sure that the staff is in compliance. Remember, we want to educate rather than discipline.

The second topic on reviewing the quarterly audit should be one of the following:

1. Everyone has done a great job and we have been successful at maintaining our core value of data security.
2. For the most part, everyone has done a great job, but we had a few items arise in the audit that need addressed.
3. There have been several issues found in the audit and we feel that re-orientation is a good option to make sure that everyone understands the procedures and why they are in place.

Ideally, we hope we the first response is the one that is used, but issues do arise from time to time and they need to be addressed. When discussing issues, do not call out names or departments. If one individual fails, we have collectively failed at reaching our goals. Use this time to discuss the items found in the audit, why they must be addressed, and steps to remedy the issue.

In my time spent managing companies, teams, and groups of people, I have found that the best way to address a problem is usually by doing it throughout the organization. It insures that others are aware and educated in addition to not alienating any one person.

The third response is the one that everyone can avoid, but if the audit shows several items across the organization that need to be addressed, reorientation may be the best option.

In Chapter 7 and 8, we discussed revision history. The next part of your quarterly meeting should be discussing any revisions that were made, when they will go into effect, and why these changes are important. During this portion of the meeting, I would recommend having staff sign off on acknowledging and accepting the revisions that were made to the security policy and update the table we made in Chapter 6, Figure 6d, to reflect the new date for policy acceptance.

The fourth point of discussion is any external threats in which the team needs to be aware. This could be from news media or data breaches at other organizations. If I was presenting this to a team today, I would go over attachments from vendors or customers that you were not expecting. Many malware programs have been hijacking contact lists and sending attachments with malware.

The email may seem legit, but if you were not expecting an attachment from the sender, call them to verify. There is always some form of malware or data breach affecting an organization somewhere and this could also be an opportunity to talk about why those businesses had the breaches and how your company's data security policies have protected your company.

Finally always ask for feedback. Your audience may point out an issue that was not found in the security audit or bring another matter of security to attention. No matter the organization, good communication with your team is the key to success.

CHAPTER 11

CLOSING REMARKS

I first want to congratulate you on finishing this book and hope that you were able to find some value in it for your business. I also want to thank you for seeing the value for establishing a core value of data security. Every day, we learn of another business that had a data breach. Our government has also not been immune and has been subjected to multiple data breaches from various branches. Those that wish to gain access to our information both internally and externally will not stop in their attempts. The frequency of data breaches is expanding at an exponential level.

As a society, what we need to do is work together to ensure that our data is safe. Just like in Chapter 10 where we talk to our staff about data security being a team effort, it is a team effort for businesses and organizations to come together as well. To protect ourselves, we all need to change the way we look at privacy, security, and data protection. Until then, the statistics will continue to climb and the billions if not trillions lost each year in breaches will continue to grow.

If you learned something from this book, please encourage your colleagues and friends at other organizations to purchase and read it as well.

Data security is a team effort and it takes all of us working towards this goal to make it a reality.

www.ingramcontent.com/pod-product-compliance
Lightning Source LLC
Chambersburg PA
CBHW060950050326

40689CB00012B/2620